Francis Frith's

Kent
Living Memories

PHOTOGRAPHIC MEMORIES

Francis Frith's
Kent
Living Memories

Keith Howell

FRITH
BOOK Co

First published in the United Kingdom in 2000 by
Frith Book Company Ltd

British Library Cataloguing in Publication Data

Kent Living Memories
Keith Howell
ISBN 1-85937-125-6

Frith Book Company Ltd
Frith's Barn, Teffont,
Salisbury, Wiltshire SP3 5QP
Tel: +44 (0) 1722 716 376
Email: info@frithbook.co.uk
www.frithbook.co.uk

Printed and bound in Great Britain

Front Cover: Faversham, Preston Street c1955 F13019

AS WITH ANY HISTORICAL DATABASE THE FRITH ARCHIVE IS CONSTANTLY BEING CORRECTED AND IMPROVED
AND THE PUBLISHERS WOULD WELCOME INFORMATION ON OMISSIONS OR INACCURACIES

Contents

Francis Frith: *Victorian Pioneer*

FRANCIS FRITH, Victorian founder of the world-famous photographic archive, was a complex and multitudinous man. A devout Quaker and a highly successful Victorian businessman, he was both philosophic by nature and pioneering in outlook.

By 1855 Francis Frith had already established a wholesale grocery business in Liverpool, and sold it for the astonishing sum of £200,000, which is the equivalent today of over £15,000,000. Now a multi-millionaire, he was able to indulge his passion for travel. As a child he had pored over travel books written by early explorers, and his fancy and imagination had been stirred by family holidays to the sublime mountain regions of Wales and Scotland. 'What a land of spirit-stirring and enriching scenes and places!' he had written. He was to return to these scenes of grandeur in later years to 'recapture the thousands of vivid and tender memories', but with a different purpose. Now in his thirties, and captivated by the new science of photography, Frith set out on a series of pioneering journeys to the Nile regions that occupied him from 1856 until 1860.

Intrigue and Adventure

He took with him on his travels a specially-designed wicker carriage that acted as both dark-room and sleeping chamber. These far-flung journeys were packed with intrigue and adventure. In his life story, written when he was sixty-three, Frith tells of being held captive by bandits, and of fighting 'an awful midnight battle to the very point of surrender with a deadly pack of hungry, wild dogs'. Sporting flowing Arab costume, Frith arrived at Akaba by camel seventy years before Lawrence, where he encountered 'desert princes and rival sheikhs, blazing with jewel-hilted swords'.

During these extraordinary adventures he was assiduously exploring the desert regions bordering the Nile and patiently recording the antiquities and peoples with his camera. He was the first photographer to venture beyond the sixth cataract. Africa was still the mysterious 'Dark Continent', and Stanley and Livingstone's historic meeting was a decade into the future. The conditions for picture taking confound belief. He laboured for hours in his wicker dark-room in the sweltering heat of the desert, while the volatile chemicals fizzed dangerously in their trays. Often he was forced to work in remote tombs and caves where conditions were cooler. Back in London he exhibited his photographs and was 'rapturously cheered' by members of the Royal Society. His reputation as a photographer was made overnight. An eminent modern historian has likened their impact on the population of the time to that on our own generation of the first photographs taken on the surface of the moon.

Venture of a Life-Time

Characteristically, Frith quickly spotted the opportunity to create a new business as a specialist publisher of photographs. He lived in an era of immense and sometimes violent change. For the poor in the early part of Victoria's reign work was a drudge and the hours long, and people had precious little free time to enjoy themselves. Most had no transport other than a cart or gig at their disposal, and had not travelled far beyond the boundaries of their own town or village.

However, by the 1870s, the railways had threaded their way across the country, and Bank Holidays and half-day Saturdays had been made obligatory by Act of Parliament. All of a sudden the ordinary working man and his family were able to enjoy days out and see a little more of the world.

With characteristic business acumen, Francis Frith foresaw that these new tourists would enjoy having souvenirs to commemorate their days out. In 1860 he married Mary Ann Rosling and set out with the intention of photographing every city, town and village in Britain. For the next thirty years he travelled the country by train and by pony and trap, producing fine photographs of seaside resorts and beauty spots that were keenly bought by millions of Victorians. These prints were painstakingly pasted into family albums and pored over during the dark nights of winter, rekindling precious memories of summer excursions.

The Rise of Frith & Co

Frith's studio was soon supplying retail shops all over the country. To meet the demand he gathered about him a small team of photographers, and published the work of independent artist-photographers of the calibre of Roger Fenton and Francis Bedford. In order to gain some understanding of the scale of Frith's business one only has to look at the catalogue issued by Frith & Co in 1886: it runs to some 670 pages, listing not only many thousands of views of the British Isles but also many photographs of most European countries, and China, Japan, the USA and Canada – note the sample page shown above

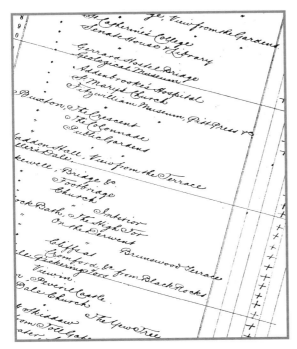

from the hand-written *Frith & Co* ledgers detailing pictures taken. By 1890 Frith had created the greatest specialist photographic publishing company in the world, with over 2,000 outlets – more than the combined number that Boots and WH Smith have today! The picture on the right shows the *Frith & Co* display board at Ingleton in the Yorkshire Dales. Beautifully constructed with mahogany frame and gilt inserts, it could display up to a dozen local scenes.

Postcard Bonanza

The ever-popular holiday postcard we know today took many years to develop. In 1870 the Post Office issued the first plain cards, with a pre-printed stamp on one face. In 1894 they allowed other publishers' cards to be sent through the mail with an attached adhesive halfpenny stamp. Demand grew rapidly, and in 1895 a new size of postcard was permitted

called the court card, but there was little room for illustration. In 1899, a year after Frith's death, a new card measuring 5.5 x 3.5 inches became the standard format, but it was not until 1902 that the divided back came into being, with address and message on one face and a full-size illustration on the other. *Frith & Co* were in the vanguard of postcard development, and Frith's sons Eustace and Cyril continued their father's monumental task, expanding the number of views offered to the public and recording more and more places in Britain, as the coasts and countryside were opened up to mass travel.

Francis Frith died in 1898 at his villa in Cannes, his great project still growing. The archive he created continued in business for another seventy years. By 1970 it contained over a third of a million pictures of 7,000 cities, towns and villages. The massive photographic record Frith has left to us stands as a living monument to a special and very remarkable man.

Frith's Archive: *A Unique Legacy*

FRANCIS FRITH'S legacy to us today is of immense significance and value, for the magnificent archive of evocative photographs he created provides a unique record of change in 7,000 cities, towns and villages throughout Britain over a century and more. Frith and his fellow studio photographers revisited locations many times down the years to update their views, compiling for us an enthralling and colourful pageant of British life and character.

We tend to think of Frith's sepia views of Britain as nostalgic, for most of us use them to conjure up memories of places in our own lives with which we have family associations. It often makes us forget that to Francis Frith they were records of daily life as it was actually being lived in the cities, towns and villages of his day. The Victorian age was one of great and often bewildering change for ordinary people, and though the pictures evoke an impression of slower times, life was as busy and hectic as it is today.

We are fortunate that Frith was a photographer of the people, dedicated to recording the minutiae of everyday life. For it is this sheer wealth of visual data, the painstaking chronicle of changes in dress, transport, street layouts, buildings, housing, engineering and landscape that captivates us so much today. His remarkable images offer us a powerful link with the past and with the lives of our ancestors.

Today's Technology

Computers have now made it possible for Frith's many thousands of images to be accessed almost instantly. In the Frith archive today, each photograph is carefully 'digitised' then stored on a CD Rom. Frith archivists can locate a single photograph amongst thousands within seconds. Views can be catalogued and sorted under a variety of categories of place and content to the immediate benefit of researchers.

Inexpensive reference prints can be created for them at the touch of a mouse button, and a wide range of books and other printed materials assembled and published for a wider, more general readership - in the next twelve months over a hundred Frith local history titles will be published! The day-to-day workings of the archive are very different from how they were in Francis Frith's time: imagine the herculean task of sorting through eleven tons of glass negatives as Frith had to do to locate a

See Frith at www. frithbook.co.uk

particular sequence of pictures! Yet the archive still prides itself on maintaining the same high standards of excellence laid down by Francis Frith, including the painstaking cataloguing and indexing of every view.

It is curious to reflect on how the internet now allows researchers in America and elsewhere greater instant access to the archive than Frith himself ever enjoyed. Many thousands of individual views can be called up on screen within seconds on one of the Frith internet sites, enabling people living continents away to revisit the streets of their ancestral home town, or view places in Britain where they have enjoyed holidays. Many overseas researchers welcome the chance to view special theme selections, such as transport, sports, costume and ancient monuments.

We are certain that Francis Frith would have heartily approved of these modern developments in imaging techniques, for he himself was always working at the very limits of Victorian photographic technology.

The Value of the Archive Today

Because of the benefits brought by the computer, Frith's images are increasingly studied by social historians, by researchers into genealogy and ancestory, by architects, town planners, and by teachers and schoolchildren involved in local history projects.

In addition, the archive offers every one of us an opportunity to examine the places where we and our families have lived and worked down the years. Highly successful in Frith's own era, the archive is now, a century and more on, entering a new phase of popularity.

The Past in Tune with the Future

Historians consider the Francis Frith Collection to be of prime national importance. It is the only archive of its kind remaining in private ownership and has been valued at a million pounds. However, this figure is now rapidly increasing as digital technology enables more and more people around the world to enjoy its benefits.

Francis Frith's archive is now housed in an historic timber barn in the beautiful village of Teffont in Wiltshire. Its founder would not recognize the archive office as it is today. In place of the many thousands of dusty boxes containing glass plate negatives and an all-pervading odour of photographic chemicals, there are now ranks of computer screens. He would be amazed to watch his images travelling round the world at unimaginable speeds through network and internet lines.

The archive's future is both bright and exciting. Francis Frith, with his unshakeable belief in making photographs available to the greatest number of people, would undoubtedly approve of what is being done today with his lifetime's work. His photographs, depicting our shared past, are now bringing pleasure and enlightenment to millions around the world a century and more after his death.

Kent Living Memories
An Introduction

" Kent, sir! Everybody knows Kent - apples, cherries, hops and women."

Mr Jingle in Pickwick Papers.

When Charles Dickens began to write his immortal comic serial in 1836, Kent could fully justify its reputation as 'the Garden of England'; the small towns and villages of the county were primarily concerned with their agricultural activities, and large scale industry and modern transport had yet to make an impact on what was essentially a rural environment.

But, within the space of a mere decade or so, the technical and scientific advances of the Victorian era were to begin to effect indelible economic and social changes on this largely pastoral scene. As with the other Home Counties surrounding London it was initially the coming of the railways which was to have the greatest impact on the subsequent development of the county and its inhabitants. The South-Eastern Railway opened its main line from Redhill to Ashford in 1842, with extensions to Dover and Margate via Canterbury following on quickly. Its rival company, the

London, Chatham and Dover Railway stimulated the growth of the Medway towns, as well as boosting holiday traffic to the newly expanding resorts along the coast. Even more importantly, towards the end of the nineteenth century, it was the railway commuter, whose daily peregrinations between the capital city and his rural home in Kent or the rapidly growing outer suburbs of London were to become such a notable feature of twentieth century life, who had the most impact on the transformation of Kent. The mushrooming of new housing developments, shops, offices and schools was initially apparent in the north and west of the county but gradually, over succeeding decades, spread across the entire region.

Also, during the second half of the nineteenth century, Kent shared in the national depression which afflicted agriculture, mainly caused by increasing food imports from America and Europe. The staple crops had been hops, fruit and sheep rather than arable farming, and although hop production reached a peak in 1878 before embarking on a gradual decline, they still remained the county's principal crop. But by 1901 only eight per cent of the employed population was still occupied on the land while, in comparison, another thirteen per cent were engaged in various forms of domestic service. Even so, the latter group was more than double the size of those engaged in the construction industry at that time, and more than three times greater than those involved in the field of engineering.

Paper-making, which had been a Kentish industry since its first arrival in Britain, continued to flourish within the county at the end of the nineteenth century, and increased with the opening of massive new mills at Dartford, Northfleet and Kemsley. Concurrently, cement production around Gravesend and along the tidal Medway expanded to become the county's biggest single industry, ravaging the landscape with its workings. That same period also saw the start of coal-mining on a substantial scale in the east of Kent, largely as a result of the abortive attempts to construct an early Channel Tunnel, which had come to an abrupt end in 1882.

This, then, was the situation in the closing years of Queen Victoria's reign and the period leading up to the First World War. You'll find a similar selection of photographs from that era in the companion volume Victorian and Edwardian Kent, and they offer a fascinating and revealing comparison to those reproduced here, which date from half a century later. The greatest and most apparent change, aside from those in everyday dress, is the enormous impact that has resulted from the introduction of the internal combustion engine to agriculture and road transport. In 1910, there were only 23,000 motor vehicles registered in the whole of Britain and, not surprisingly, in none of the pictures in the previous collection is there any sign of their existence. Every single vehicle is horse-drawn and, outside of the major centres of population, all the roads are unsurfaced.

But, within the space of less than fifty years, the motor car had wreaked an amazing transformation not only on the Kent landscape but also on the pace of daily existence: a process which continues unabated up to the present day. And the photographs in this book, of course, precede the construction of the M2, M20 and M25 motorways that now scythe through the Kent countryside and the building of many of the new bypasses around the towns and villages in the county. Nevertheless, the process of gradual urbanisation of the county in the mid-twentieth century, along with its accompanying industrialisation, is clearly apparent in these pages.

Kent's other soubriquet, 'the Gateway to England', had no less relevance in the mid-1900s than it had in previous centuries. Ever since the days of the Roman invasions, the county had always been the first place of contact for those travelling to England and the embarkation point for those departing to the European continent. Though modern air travel, via Britain's major airports, had alleviated some of this traffic through Dover, Ramsgate and Folkestone in the middle of the last century, the undertaking of the huge Channel Tunnel project, with its accompanying infrastructure, again placed increased demands on the county's landscape and resources. These will be further supplemented over the next decade as the building of the £5 billion Channel Tunnel Rail Link takes place, making Kent more of a conduit than a county.

Even so, in spite of all these changes and with further development continuing at an ever-accelerating pace, there are still many parts of Kent which are essentially little changed.

Mr Jingle, and his eminent creator, might well be disconcerted and puzzled by many of the innovations that have come into existence in the county over the past hundred and fifty years, but they would undoubtedly still be able to recognise, as will you, many of the places which are represented within these pages.

Canterbury & The East Coast

BROADSTAIRS c1960 B220015
Broadstairs was the queen of all watering places as far as Charles
Dickens was concerned; he first visited here in 1837, and
subsequently wrote 'Nicholas Nickleby', 'Barnaby Rug', 'The
Pickwick Papers' and 'The Old Curiosity Shop' while staying in
rented houses in this rapidly-growing resort. Much of 'David
Copperfield' was penned in the crenellated Fort House, visible on
the left, which has been renamed Bleak House and is now
a commemorative museum.

BROADSTAIRS, YORK GATE c1960 B220024
This 16th-century arch, leading from the original village down to the harbour, was once fitted with a portcullis and gates as a protection for the settlement against pirates and sea-raiders. It was narrowly saved from demolition in the 19th century, and has been incorporated into subsequent buildings.

MONKTON, THE POST OFFICE c1955 M257010

With its wall-mounted Victorian letterbox, modern telephone box, and window display of assorted goods, this little post office was of central importance to the daily lives of the inhabitants of this small hamlet on the River Stour. Around the time of the first millennium, a Saxon queen donated the settlement to the monks of Christ Church, Canterbury.

MINSTER-IN-THANET, THE SQUARE c1955 M86020

One of the earliest centres of Christianity in Kent, this village, with its main street and small shops running down to the large 12th-century Norman church on the left, was the site of a nunnery founded in AD 669 by Domneva, on ten thousand acres of land given to her by King Egbert.

LITTLEBOURNE, HIGH STREET c1955 L56001

Littlebourne is one of the charming villages which are scattered throughout the orchard-rich swathe of countryside which reaches between Canterbury and Wingham. Its two public houses, the Anchor and the King William, are at the end of a long street whose buildings present an intriguing mix of architectural styles.

ICKHAM, THE MILL c1955 I1019

The mill pond at Ickham, on the east bank of the Little Stour, is crossed by this seemingly fragile footbridge whose supporting piles serve as a useful trap for waterweeds and other detritus before the stream moves on to power the wheel inside the shed.

ASH-BY-SANDWICH, THE STREET c1955 A232027

There is a cosy feel to the main street of this little village, between Sandwich and Wingham; it centres around the local shop, the Chequers Inn (on the extreme right) and the brick-built bus shelter. A parked lorry, with its driver's door open, is delivering supplies of bottled gas or paraffin to the local store.

SANDWICH, THE BARBICAN c1955 S60018

Across the sluggish waters of the River Stour, the Bridgegate, usually called the Barbican, was built in 1539 with semi-circular flanking bastions. It still carries northbound traffic out of the town towards Ramsgate. On the extreme left is the Bell Hotel, situated on the Quay.

EASTRY, HIGH STREET c1960 E154006

Between Canterbury and the sea, and built on a section of the Roman road which ran from Dover to Richborough, Eastry was once the site of a palace of the Kings of Kent, who divided their realm into 'lathes'. Thomas a Becket hid in the village before embarking on his secret flight to France in 1164.

CANTERBURY, GENERAL VIEW c1953 C18003

This view was photographed from the tower of the Westgate. The vast bulk of the Cathedral soars above the city, and St Peter's Street and the High Street are seen bedecked in flags and bunting to mark the coronation of Queen Elizabeth the Second. The small towers of St Peter's Church and St George's Church are visible on the left-hand side of the thoroughfare.

CANTERBURY, ST DUNSTAN'S STREET c1955 C18047
The massive twin-towered Westgate is the only survivor of the six medieval gates which once interrupted the path of the Norman wall around the city. The rest were pulled down in 1781. It was rebuilt in about 1380 for Archbishop Simon of Sudbury. Until 1829 it was the city jail, but in 1906 it became a museum of arms and armour.

CANTERBURY, ST PETER'S STREET c1955 C18041
As we look from inside the city walls through the arch to St Dunstan's Street, we can see the route taken by Henry II when he came as a penitent after the murder of Thomas Becket in 1174, and by Henry V on his triumphal return from Agincourt. In 1859, a menagerie owner petitioned the city corporation to be allowed to pull the Westgate down in order to gain access for his performing elephants. Voting was evenly divided between the councillors, but the mayor's casting vote saved the structure from demolition.

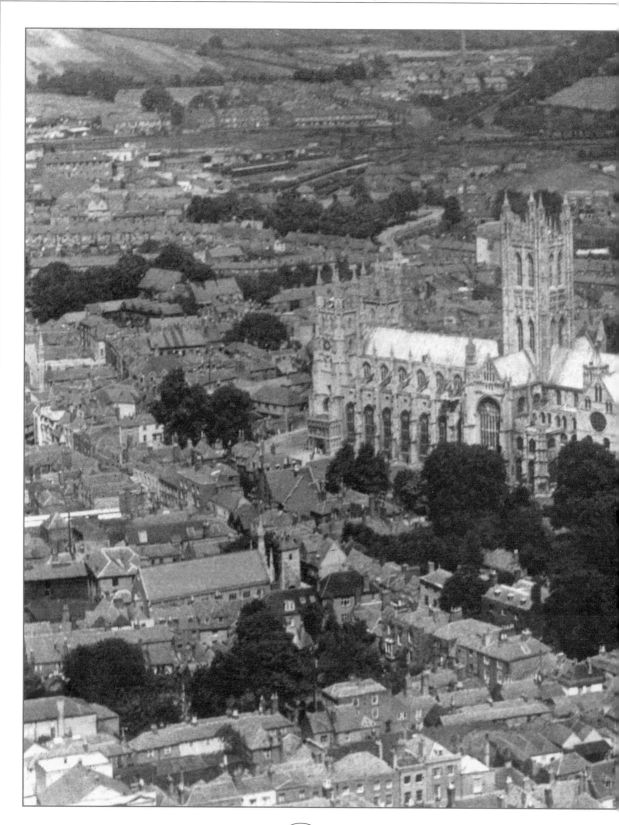

CANTERBURY
THE CATHEDRAL FROM THE AIR c1955
C18061

Dwarfing the surrounding buildings, the 43,000 square feet of England's mother-church and the seat of the Primate of All England is revealed in all its architectural glory from this unusual vantage point. Ninth in size amongst the English cathedrals, with a total interior length of 517 feet and its central tower ascending to 235 feet, it is still one of Europe's most celebrated places of Christian pilgrimage.

CANTERBURY, MERCERY LANE c1955 C18027

Leading to the cathedral, this narrow alleyway with its overhanging shop fronts was the usual route by which pilgrims approached the climax of their journey. It would have been lined with shops and stalls selling religious medallions, phials of water from Becket's Well in the cathedral crypt and other memorabilia; the lane still conveys much of its medieval atmosphere, particularly when decorated with evergreens as in this photograph.

CANTERBURY
High Street c1955 C18079
Above the modern shopfronts and advertising signs,
the picturesque assortment of buildings bear
testimony to the city's rich history. Across the street
is the entrance to Mercery Lane, with the
overhanging beams of a former pilgrims' inn, the
Chequer of Hope, which once stretched back to the
Buttermarket. On the right, with a branch of
Barclay's Bank on the corner, is Stour Street.

NONINGTON, THE CHURCH c1955 N142089

A timbered barn stands opposite the entrance to this 13th-century church with its small square crenellated tower. The village boasted two large houses, Fredville and St Alban's Court, whose family members lie buried in the small chapels inside.

DEAL, THE CASTLE c1955 D15041

This was the largest of three fortresses built by Henry VIII in 1538 to protect this stretch of Kent coast against the threat of invasion by Francois I of France. Six semi-circular bastions fan out from a round central keep, all surrounded by a massive moat. Although its defences were never tested by a foreign invader, during the Second World War the Germans succeeded in scoring a direct hit on the structure.

DEAL
High Street c1955 D15020
This main street runs parallel to the shore, and displays many of the late 19th-century shops that accompanied its development as a resort during that period. Earlier, William Cobbett, passing through in the course of his 'Rural Rides', described it as 'a villainous place full of filthy looking people'.

EYTHORNE, CHAPEL HILL c1955 E158010

Along with its neighbouring villages of Betteshanger and Tilmanstone, this settlement was a centre of the short-lived Kent coal industry, which began when coal was discovered when borings for a proposed Channel tunnel were being made in 1891. The Kentish miners earned themselves a reputation for being among the most militant members of their arduous profession, before the local branch of the industry was shut down in the 1970s.

WALMER, THE VILLAGE c1955 W12001

These solid stone cottages, and the George Inn on the left, exhibit the robust and simple style which is common to most British fishing ports. Certainly the men of Walmer, who have manned the lifeboat stationed here since 1856, have good cause to regard the sea and weather with caution. They have left the security of these snug buildings in treacherous conditions to save more than eighteen hundred souls whose vessels have come to grief on the nearby Goodwin Sands over the intervening years.

DOVER, THE CASTLE c1965 D50009
One of the finest fortresses in England, Dover Castle traces its history back to the Iron Age earthworks on the site. But the great keep, the inner bailey and much of the curtain walling were built by Henry II between 1168-86, at the then colossal cost of £3,000. Further additions to the defences were made by Henry III, and also during the Napoleonic Wars, and again in the Second World War.

DOVER, MARINE PARADE c1965 D50145
With the Castle and the Saxon church of St. Mary-in-Castro 400 feet above on the cliffs behind, and the famous white cliffs receding into the distance, holidaymakers settle down to enjoy their day at the seaside. The block of modern flats on the left replaced a smaller group of houses that were destroyed by enemy action during the Second World War.

FOLKESTONE, THE HARBOUR c1955 F35050
On the left, the east pier reaches out across the harbour towards the railway station complex, with the long stone pier carrying the line continuing on towards the small lighthouse at its end. In the foreground the ornamental gardens, with their close cropped lawns and carefully tended flowerbeds of The Leas, await their daily procession of visitors and holidaymakers.

HYTHE, THE PROMENADE c1960 H141049
The broad expanse of the Promenade stretching east to Sandgate is still as popular with visitors today as it was with the Victorian and Edwardian holidaymakers who visited this Cinque Port, and whose continued presence prompted the construction of the balconied villas along this stretch of the front.

LYMPNE, THE AIRPORT c1955 L335039

The small civil airport at Lympne was developed from the wartime fighter base, prior to the enormous expansion of London's Heathrow and Gatwick airports, for short cross-channel flights. The limited scale of its operations can be gauged from the relaxed attitudes of these members of its staff as they await the next incoming flight in front of the customs and immigration shed, with a coach poised to transport the arriving passengers to the railway station at Hythe.

ELHAM, HIGH STREET c1960 E156007

The pretty village of Elham, at the heart of the valley of that name, is clustered around its market square and this High Street, lined with buildings from several periods. Some are of brick, and others are half-timbered, with their upper storeys jutting out on carved brackets. The village lies on the course of the Little Stour, a 'nailbourne' or intermittent stream, whose sporadic flow was popularly held to presage either death or disaster.

DUNGENESS, THE LIGHTHOUSE c1965 D165013
The light from the third model of 1904 was obscured by the buildings of the nearby power stations: therefore, although it still stands, it was replaced in 1961 by the taller black and white striped edifice whose Xenon electric arc lamp is visible for seventeen miles out to sea.

DUNGENESS
The Lighthouse c1965 D165011
There has been a lighthouse on
Dungeness Point since 1615, with the
circular base of its initial successor from
1792 preserved as the accommodation
of the keepers.

NEW ROMNEY
North Street c1955 N141007
Now a full mile and a half from the sea,
New Romney was, in the 13th century,
first among the five Cinque Ports. But a
great storm in 1287 diverted the River
Rother to Rye and destroyed New
Romney's harbour. It remained the seat
of the chief courts of the Cinque Ports,
and returned two members of
Parliament up until 1832.

Maidstone and the Weald

AYLESFORD

Kit's Coty House c1960 A85040

One of the most famous prehistoric structures in England, these three upright stones, surmounted by a capstone almost thirteen feet long, formed the central compartment of a Neolithic burial chamber. They were once covered with a mound of earth, but this has been eroded away. The name is possibly derived from the Celtic 'ked koit', the tomb in the wood.

AYLESFORD, FROM THE RIVERWALK c1960 A85001

This settlement commanded the lowest fording point on the River Medway, and here, in 455, the invading Jutes under Hengist defeated the native forces led by Vortigern. Pilgrims on their way to Becket's shrine at Canterbury must also have crossed the river here. The bridge is the oldest on the Medway, dating back to the 14th century, but the central span was enlarged in the 19th century to accommodate the increasing traffic on the river.

ALLINGTON, THE CASTLE c1965 A230023

Enclosed by a bend in the river Medway, the castle was founded in early Norman times and rebuilt during the late 13th century by Sir Stephen de Penchester, a Warden of the Cinque Ports. The eminent mountaineer Lord Conway again extensively restored the buildings between 1906-32. Since 1951, the castle has been occupied by an order of Carmelite nuns.

ALLINGTON, THE LOCKS c1965 A230037

At this point the River Medway ceases to be tidal; the electrical sluice gates here, thirty feet wide and fifteen feet deep, are an essential part of the flood control scheme of the Medway Valley. Installed in 1930, they can discharge three million gallons of water a day and are operated by a switch. Locally-quarried stone was transported from here to London by barge as far back as Roman and Norman times.

MAIDSTONE, THE RIVER MEDWAY AND THE CHURCH c1955 M9018

This view looks south from the bridge over the River Medway. The lofty tower of the 14th-century All Saints church rises behind the Archbishop's Manor House and grounds. Originally built by Archbishop Islip in the mid 14th century, it was subsequently altered by Archbishop Morton during the following century. Its panelled banqueting room is nowadays used for lectures and meetings.

MAIDSTONE, THE ZOO PARK c1955 M9030
Situated in the 270-acre grounds of Cobtree Manor, an Elizabethan house alleged to be the original of Mr Wardell's Dingley Dell in 'Pickwick Papers', this formerly popular family attraction was noted for its polar bears and lions, but it closed a few years after this photograph was taken. The park is now partly occupied by a golf course, picnic sites and nature trails.

MAIDSTONE, HIGH STREET c1955 M9063
At the bottom of Maidstone High Street both the Queen's Head public house, on the left, and the Rose and Crown Hotel across the road have gone; the trolleybuses also went in 1966. The soldier marching smartly across the road is almost certainly a member of the Queen's Own Royal West Kent Regiment, garrisoned here. The cannon, mounted on its plinth, is still in situ, and is now joined in the summer months by a floral sheep.

MAIDSTONE
HIGH STREET c1955 M9004
A positive cats-cradle of wires weaves above the roadway, with telephone cables, suspended street lighting and the power cables for the silent-running electric trolley buses contesting the airspace. As the county and assize town of Kent, as well as its chief agricultural centre, Maidstone is also a busy market and shopping centre, and many of its older buildings are overshadowed by the commercial activity.

LEEDS CASTLE c1955 L29077

Originally a wooden Saxon fortress built on two islands, the building was transformed into a solid stone castle at the end of the 12th century by the Norman baron Robert de Crevecoeur. Over three centuries it was the dower home of eight medieval queens in succession. Henry VIII lavished substantial sums on its improvement, before it passed into the possession of the St Leger, Culpeper and Fairfax families in turn.

LENHAM, FAVERSHAM ROAD c1955 L322006

Once an important and flourishing market on the old coach road, Lenham embodies a fine mix of building styles from medieval through to Georgian in its houses and shops. Now bypassed by the M20 motorway, half a mile away, it has been able to regain some semblance of its former tranquillity.

CHILHAM, THE CASTLE c1955 C90006

This brick Jacobean mansion was built in 1616 for Sir Dudley Digges, a Master of the Rolls, and is claimed to be to the design of Inigo Jones. The terraced and topiary gardens contain the first wisteria and mulberry ever to be planted in Britain, and were landscaped by Capability Brown and John Tradescant.

CHILHAM, HIGH STREET c1955 C90024

Pollarded lime trees line part of the High Street of this village, which can justifiably claim to be one of Kent's prettiest; it duly attracts hordes of visitors during the summer season. Set in the valley of the River Stour, its Tudor and Jacobean houses have been carefully maintained, and further up the street is the old Woolpack Inn.

CHARING, THE CHURCH c1955 C60001

On the left are the remains of the Archbishop's Palace, or manor house, where Archbishop Warham entertained Henry VII in 1507, and where Henry VIII stayed in 1520 when he was on his way to the Field of the Cloth of Gold. The body of the church, mainly 15th-century, is older than its Perpendicular tower, which is a local landmark.

CHARING, HIGH STREET c1955 C60027

On the right, the village shop and bus stop, as always, provide a meeting place for members of this community. On the left-hand side of the street is the village teashop, next door to the bakery with its metal advertising signs for Hovis and Vitbe bread.

ASHFORD
High Street c1950 A71010

A bustling agricultural town and a centre of
communications, Ashford was already undergoing a
process of extensive and rapid change by the 1950s.
Its central High Street, though still recognisably
Georgian in character above ground level, was
seeing the introduction of modern shopfronts and
advertising signs.

ASHFORD, HIGH STREET c1955 A71064
The broad expanse of what had been
Ashford's original market place and a
rendezvous for Kent's sheep and cattle
farmers had, by the mid 1950s, been
bisected by a central traffic reservation
and new road markings. Concealed
from view behind the shops on the left
is the landmark Perpendicular tower of
the church.

PLUCKLEY, THE SQUARE c1955 P57025
Standing on a steep hillside north-west of Ashford, and with commanding views of the Weald, this charming village was near the seat of the Dering family. It is their black horse insignia which is displayed on the pub sign of the Dering Arms.

WYE, CHURCH STREET c1955 W157010
Standing above the east bank of the river Stour, Wye was a royal manor before the Norman Conquest, and was given by William I to Battle Abbey in Susses. The church was rebuilt in 1447, and the nave of that building forms part of the present structure, but in 1686 the original steeple fell, destroying the chancel and its aisles. A new chancel and the low square tower were provided.

BROOK, THE CHURCH c1955 B583012

Three miles from Wye, the Norman village church has remained largely unaltered since it was built, with the exception of its windows. The large square tower was restored after it was struck by lightning in 1896. The little stream, in the immediate foreground, gives the village its name.

BETHERSDEN, FORGE HILL c1955 B571004

A typical village of the Kent Weald, with its weatherboarded cottages clustered round its green, Bethersden was once famous for its paludrina marble extracted from the local clay and consisting of the fossilised shells of a freshwater snail. It was used to adorn the cathedrals of Canterbury and Rochester.

SMARDEN, THE STREET C1955 S533032
Smarden is one of Kent's most beautiful villages; its name derives from the Saxon 'smeredaenne', meaning 'butter valley and pasture'. It is built on a dog-leg construction and lined with half-timbered and weatherboarded cottages.

SMARDEN, THE STREET c1955 S533021

The weatherboarded Chequers pub is tucked away in a corner of the dog-leg at the top of the village street, with the early 15th-century church tower rising above the surrounding tiled roofs. It is known as 'the barn of Kent' because of the width of its aisleless nave and the timber scissor-beam roof.

BIDDENDEN, THE VILLAGE c1960 B88004

Most of the delightful old houses along this street were constructed during the 15th century, at a time when the village prospered as part of the profitable cloth trade centred on Cranbrook. Each Easter Monday it still celebrates the memory of the 'Maids of Biddenden', two Tudor Siamese twins joined at the hips and shoulders who lived for thirty-four years.

HIGH HALDEN, THE CHURCH c1955 H354022

Once surrounded by forested land, this church boasts remarkable timbered west and south porches built in the early 14th century, and comprising some fifty tons of oak wood. The tower, also timbered, is unique in the county.

APPLEDORE, THE VILLAGE c1955 A231010

On the edge of Romney Marsh, this village, with its broad street, was once a flourishing seaport and shipbuilding centre; it was captured by the Danes with a fleet of 250 ships in the 9th century. But the great storm of 1287 altered the course of the River Rother, and Appledore then developed as a market town, although its last fair was held in 1899.

GOUDHURST, THE STAR AND EAGLE c1955 G38062
Standing near the top of a hill overlooking the Weald, the Star and Eagle is a fine half-timbered 15th-century inn adjoining the churchyard, and is believed to have had monastic connections. Next door is the weather-boarded Eight Bells.

GOUDHURST, THE CHURCH c1955 G38303
The top of the tower of this 13th-century church is five hundred feet above sea level, and was used as a lookout point in both world wars. An earlier medieval tower was destroyed in a storm in 1637. The building was the scene of an epic battle involving the local militia and the Hawkhurst gang of smugglers in 1747.

CRANBROOK, THE VILLAGE c1960 C178022
The sails of the Union Windmill peep over the roofs of the half-timbered cottages lining the street. Built in 1814 for Henry Dobell, the mill received its name because a union of local tradesmen ran it. In the 14th century, Cranbrook became the centre of cloth making in the county after Edward III lured Flemish weavers to settle here. The trade lasted until the 18th century.

LAMBERHURST, THE VILLAGE c1960 L323007
Lamberhurst was an ironworking centre between the 16th and the 18th centuries. The local industry used charcoal from the great woodlands around the area, and water power from the River Teise on which the village stands. Parts of the railings surrounding St Paul's Cathedral were made here, and a section of the balustrade still stands outside the village hall.

North Kent

GRAVESEND
New Road c1955 G47003
Here we see shoppers in the centre of town on what was obviously
a warm summer's morning, and with a surprisingly low level of
traffic. Behind the parked car on the left, the striped awning
protects a tobacconist's display from the sun, while next door is the
extensive frontage of the British Home Stores, with the offices of
the Pearl Assurance Company above.

GRAVESEND

THE CLOCK TOWER c1955 G47009

John Johnson's imposing Gothic clock tower, built in 1887 of white stone with sporadic red bands and gabled clock faces, was originally intended to form the centrepiece of a new building development, some of which surrounds it in Berkeley Crescent, behind. Now it provides a focal point for the start of the town's main shopping street.

GRAVESEND
HIGH STREET c1955 G47020
The excessively narrow High Street runs down to the town pier and the passenger ferry across the River Thames to Tilbury.

GRAVESEND
HIGH STREET c1955 G47010
The High Street's shabby Victorian buildings and wide variety of shops have been familiar to generations of holidaymakers and tourists on coming ashore. In the mid-fifties, lighting for the street was provided by electric lamps suspended above the carriageway.

GRAVESEND, THE HARBOUR c1955 G47012

A tender crewed by two men prepares to cast off from the jetty; beyond, this busy reach of the River Thames is crowded with an assortment of vessels preparing either to take on river pilots for the twenty-six mile journey upstream to the Port of London, or deep-sea pilots for their exit from the estuary.

GRAVESEND, THE TILBURY FERRY c1955 G47053

The passenger ferry from the Essex port of Tilbury approaches the Town Pier at the end of its journey across the Thames. The service operated daily from around five in the morning until midnight, with return tickets costing less than a shilling (5 pence).

ROCHESTER, COLLEGE GATE C1965 R44168
One of the three surviving 15th-century entrances to the cathedral precincts, College Gate stands at the foot of Boley Hill, and is banded with stone and flint, with a timber-framed upper storey. Charles Dickens incorporated it in his novel 'Edwin Drood' as Jasper's Gate.

ROCHESTER
THE CATHEDRAL c1955 R44159

Rochester is one of the smallest English cathedrals, measuring 23,300 square feet in area. It was built mainly in the 12th to the 14th centuries, but exhibits work of every period down to the present day. Like Canterbury, it is unusual in having double transepts, along with a raised choir and presbytery with a large crypt beneath. The central tower and spire rise to a height of 156 feet, and were originally completed in 1343 by Bishop Hamo de Hythe. They were rebuilt in the 19th century and again in 1904. At the time this photograph was taken, the building was again undergoing restoration.

ROCHESTER, THE BRIDGE c1955 R44040

The iron bridge, raised in 1914, carries the London road over the River Medway into Rochester; it replaced the old stone bridge, which had stood a little further upstream by the Bridge Chapel. It was demolished in 1856, having been constructed between 1387-92 by two knights who had enriched themselves in the service of the Black Prince.

ROCHESTER, HIGH STREET c1955 R44034

Among the many old buildings in this stretch of the High Street is the Tudor brick Eastgate House, seen on the right, and now the Charles Dickens Centre. The interior is laid out in a series of tableaux depicting scenes from the lives of his characters, while in the garden is the Swiss chalet which the author had imported to the grounds of his home at Gads Hill.

ROCHESTER
High Street c1955 R44033

The policeman on point duty at the busy junction of the High Street, Eastgate, and Star Hill stands in the seemingly flimsy protection of a small, wheeled cubicle to carry out his duties of directing the traffic. Members of today's constabulary are no doubt grateful that this task is now carried out by automatic traffic lights.

SNODLAND, THE RAILWAY STATION C1965 S535030

This industrial village on the outskirts of Rochester, now surrounded by cement works and paper mills, was the site of famous vineyards in the 14th century. So perhaps it is appropriate that its classically-styled railway station might almost have been transported here direct from France.

SNODLAND, HIGH STREET c1965 S535020

The narrow High Street, with its branch of the National Provincial Bank (later to become the National Westminster Bank) on the right, and the local Post Office, shoe-shop, and newsagents on the left, was bedevilled by the heavy traffic from the local cement works. Major roadworks, and the building of a by-pass in the 1980s, have helped to resolve the problem.

RAINHAM, FISHERMEN BY THE RIVER c1960 R80044

As the River Medway slowly winds its way to Sheerness and the Thames estuary, the land becomes marshier and silt-laden, as the reeds along these banks show. But the resulting nutrients which are present also attract fish and, inevitably, keen anglers.

SITTINGBOURNE
HIGH STREET c1965 S531058

Astride the A2, the old market town of Sittingbourne was an important staging point on the medieval pilgrims' route to Canterbury and, later on, in the coaching era. The 15th-century flint tower of the parish church still dominates the long street, which retains vestiges of a Georgian heritage in some of its buildings, although the Victorians were responsible for desecrating many others.

SHEERNESS, THE ESPLANADE AND THE BEACH c1955 S528048

Although there is no evidence of habitation here before the 17th century, this windswept north-west corner of the Isle of Sheppey has since enjoyed a measure of success as a seaside resort as a result of its bracing climate. The mile-and-a-half-long Esplanade, overlooking a beach of sand and shingle and with its adjacent amusement park, continues to attract visitors.

OSPRINGE, WATER LANE c1955 O25003

The Romans had a settlement here at Ospringe. On opposite corners of Water Lane are the only two buildings to survive from the Maison Dieu, one of neighbouring Faversham's three medieval religious foundations. It fulfilled several purposes, serving as hospital, almshouses and pilgrims' hostel, but the two houses were the homes of chantry priests.

FAVERSHAM, THE GUILDHALL c1960 F13016

The Guildhall was built in 1574 as a market hall; it was rebuilt in 1814, except for the splendid timber arches on which it rests, and which serve as shelter for the stall-holders and their customers. Just behind, and visible by the telephone box, is an ornate Victorian cast-iron pump.

FAVERSHAM, WEST STREET c1960 F13038

The Ship Hotel on the immediate left, with its decorated signboard and the golden cockerel trademark of Courage's brewery, was originally an Elizabethan hostelry. It was altered in the 18th century, but still retains an original Elizabethan plaster ceiling and timber beams. Almost opposite at No 121 is a plaster-fronted house bearing the date 1697.

FAVERSHAM, ABBEY STREET c1965 F13057

The lines of parked vehicles on both sides of the road tend to detract from the architectural riches of the fine Tudor, Georgian and Victorian buildings that adorn this spacious street; they are evidence of Faversham's hey-day as a branch of the Cinque port of Dover. It once housed the abbey founded by King Stephen in 1147, where he was buried with his queen Matilda. The site was excavated in 1964, and the remains of the great church, 360 feet long, can now be viewed.

FAVERSHAM
PRESTON STREET c1955 F13019
A police officer keeps a close eye on traffic at the foot of Preston Street, with the International Stores displaying its selection of groceries in its corner window, and the printers and stationer's shop of Voile and Roberson with its ornately carved entrance on the adjacent corner. Further along on the left is the hanging sign of the Prince Albert public house.

WHITSTABLE, THE HARBOUR c1955 W405008

Here we have two views of the spacious harbour, opened in 1832 as the port for Canterbury, seven miles further inland. The drying nets on the harbour wall, and a rich assortment of small fishing boats and pleasure craft moored at low water, provide evidence of the demand on its facilities.

WHITSTABLE, THE HARBOUR c1955 W405029

WHITSTABLE
Marine Terrace c1955 W405016
These trim houses with their first-floor verandas overlooking the
shingle beach and breakwaters, and the neat gardens behind their
fences, present an almost idyllic seaside vista. But when fierce
onshore winter storms arrive, as they did most devastatingly in
1953, the householders are made all too aware of their
vulnerability to the forces of nature.

TANKERTON
THE BEACH c1955 T228002
Between Whitstable and Herne Bay, this modern residential suburb and resort, with its grassy cliff-top promenade and shingle beach, was developed mainly in the years following the Second World War. As the photograph shows, it proved extremely popular with families; it also provided additional welcome income for local fishermen, one of whom is seated in the middle foreground accompanied by his faithful dog.

HERNE BAY
CENTRAL PARADE c1955
H75003

This is the central bandstand, where, according to the advertising banner, Billy Merrin & The Commanders were preparing to perform at the time of the photographer's visit. The bandstand has long been numbered among this popular resort's major entertainment attractions. It has acquired even greater prominence following the loss of the Pier Pavilion and the pier itself.

HERNE BAY, THE BEACH
c1955 H75011
Any more for the 'Skylark'? Holidaymakers queue up for the traditional offshore boat trip, while in the background the 19th-century pier steps out to sea on its spindly legs. At almost three-quarters of a mile in length, it was the second-longest pier in England after Southend's, but was damaged by a severe storm in 1978 and pulled down the following year. The Grand Pier Pavilion, opened by the Lord Mayor of London in 1910, had already been gutted by fire in 1970.

HERNE BAY
CENTRAL PARADE c1955 H75026
A local weather recording station, no doubt keeping a carefully tally of the total of sunshine hours, stands amid the formal gardens along the front. Beyond is the Central Bandstand, and rising in the distance is the landmark purpose-built clock tower donated to the town in 1837 by a wealthy widow.

HERNE BAY, c1955 H75034

A splendid example of nineteen-thirties design with its curving lines and elegant windows, this restaurant clearly retained its popularity with customers well into the fifties.

BIRCHINGTON, THE SQUARE c1955 B278002

Birchington is the westernmost of Margate's satellite villages; the old quarter of this resort is more than a half-mile from the sea front. Neat flowerbeds surround the drinking fountain with its quaint spire, while in the background, just beyond Jenner's garage and petrol pump, the name of the Smugglers public house hints at past activities of bygone residents.

West Kent

DARTFORD
High Street c1955 D3031
This photograph shows the centre of the busy High Street,
with the road to Bexley and London ahead and the turning
to Crayford visible on the right. The overhead wires powering
the trolleybus service and the numerous advertising signs add
to the general clutter of this scene. Outside the Midland
Bank, a queue of people waits patiently in the sunshine
for the next bus.

DARTFORD
THE CROWN AND ANCHOR INN c1955
D3069
This restored medieval house, on the corner of Bullace Lane, is claimed to have been the home of the Kentish rebel Wat Tyler. It was here in 1382 that an insolent tax collector insulted Tyler's daughter and was killed by Tyler with a hammer; Tyler became a people's hero.

GREENHITHE, THE RIVER c1955 G215019

Majestically dominating the scene, and surrounded by a collection of more modern cargo ships and lighters, is the Merchant Navy sail training ship HMS 'Worcester'. Specially built in 1905 for its purpose and measuring 314 feet in length, it was removed from this mooring in the late 1970s.

NORTHFLEET, THE HILL c1955 N143004

On the right, the warm, brown fletton brick tower of Sir Giles Scott's Roman Catholic church of Our Lady of the Assumption soars above the surrounding buildings lining the broad street. Built in 1914, it mirrors the outline which Scott used again when designing the central tower of Liverpool Cathedral.

NORTHFLEET, PIER ROAD C1955 N143012

Marking the point on the Thames where its estuary becomes a river, Northfleet was originally noted for its shipbuilding in the days of the great East Indiamen, but this gave way to the manufacture of cement and paper in the mid 19th century. The tall chimneys behind this graceful stone house reflect this change. But these spectators, taking advantage of the seats provided, can still look out onto the Thames and the passing river traffic.

FARNINGHAM, HIGH STREET C1960 F154025

In the 18th century, Farningham was a stopping place on the main London-Dover road, but was by-passed with the construction of the A20. The Lion Hotel, down the hill, was a grand coaching inn whose gardens run down to the River Darent. On the right, the half-timbered Post Office and the adjoining small shops sport an impressive number of modern advertising signs.

EYNSFORD, THE VILLAGE c1955 E55030

Beyond the hump-backed 15th-century bridge over the River Darent, and the adjoining ford, is a picturesque Tudor house and a line of cottages looking out onto the grassy banks. In the distance is the square flint tower of the 13th-century St Martin's church.

MEOPHAM, THE GREEN c1965 M253019

This wide triangle of grass forms the centre of this straggling village, which stretches for almost four miles. The black-painted smock windmill, set back from the road, and the prominent Cricketers pub facing the local cricket pavilion, are both local landmarks.

OTFORD, THE VILLAGE POND C1955 O87070

Weeping willows overhang the village pond and its coop for the ornamental waterfowl; they lie at the heart of a village whose history stretches back to Roman times. Across the narrow street, the whitewashed Crown Inn and the adjoining old cottages complete the picturesque scene.

KEMSING, THE VILLAGE C1955 K122007

The pretty village of Kemsing, on the Pilgrims' Way, boasts St Edith's Well, which is just by the walled war memorial at this road junction. The daughter of King Edgar the Peaceful and Lady Wulfrith, Edith was born in the village in 961, but lived most of her short life at Wilton Abbey in Wiltshire. After her death at twenty-four, a cult developed around her name, and the local priest would bless corn and other crops in her name to protect them from mildew and blight.

IGHTHAM, THE VILLAGE c1965 I4046

The half-timbered frontage of the George and Dragon inn dates from 1515, and the petrol pumps in its forecourt from the 20th century. Across the winding street, the village grocer's shop was formerly run by the noted local archaeologist Benjamin Harrison (1837- 1921), who was responsible for the discovery of numerous early flint tools in the vicinity.

SEVENOAKS, HIGH STREET c1955 S98008

Livestock was still being bought and sold in the Market Place, on the centre left of the picture, until only a few years before this picture was taken. The Chequers Inn, whose signboard is visible on the extreme left, has been in business here for almost four centuries.

SEVENOAKS, UPPER ST JOHN'S HILL c1960 S98062

St John's Church, built in 1858-9 by Morphew & Green and with its west gable-end facing out onto the road junction, dominates this cross-roads towards the top of the hill. Described by Pevsner as 'a cheap church', its northern aisle was added in 1878.

SEVENOAKS, UPPER HIGH STREET c1955 S98057

A pram and its occupant wait outside the tobacconists, with its impressive display of advertising signs, in this line of quaint overhung shops. At the extreme left is an embroidery and needlework supplier, and at the far end, just by the bend and the entrance to Six Bells Lane, is Raley & Sons' bakery offering home-made cakes and other confectionery.

**SEVENOAKS, HIGH STREET
c1960** S98065
Across the street, the mock-timbered frontage of the Holmsdale pub, with its coat of arms suspended beneath the Watney's Red Barrel advertising emblem, adjoins the similarly sham premises of Freeman, Hardy and Willis's shoe shop. On the right-hand side, Timothy White's chemist's shop boasts a cast-iron canopy over its entrance.

SEVENOAKS, HIGH STREET c1965
S98116

The solid stone structure of the Midland Bank building stands at the central junction, where the main A225 to Deptford is crossed by the A25 linking Maidstone and Westerham. The old Victorian drinking fountain with its ornate lamps stands isolated in the middle of the intersection, while on the right are branches of the International Stores and the National and Provincial Bank, shortly to be amalgamated into the National Westminster Bank.

KNOLE PARK c1960 K45003
The ancestral seat of the
Sackville family since 1603,
and one of the largest
baronial mansions in
England, Knole was
presented to the National
Trust in 1946. This
magnificent house, built of
silver-grey Kentish
ragstone, stands in one of
the most extensive and
beautiful parks in the
country, reaching up to the
Greensands Hills. It covers
about a thousand acres
and is nearly six miles in
circumference.

PLAXTOL, THE VILLAGE c1960 P56001

Commissioned by Archbishop Laud, the ragstone church stands at the centre of this lovely village, and according to an inscription over the porch's inner door it was originally built in 1649. But it was extensively altered and repaired at the end of the 19th century by Robert Pearsall, although it still retains its impressive hammerbeam roof over the nave.

BRASTED, HIGH STREET c1955 B580054

With its pollarded lime trees and some charming half-timbered cottages spread along its length, the village High Street suffered for several decades from the heavy traffic which thundered along this stretch of the A25 to Westerham, until the building of the M25 motorway brought a return to some semblance of rural tranquillity. During the Second World War, the fighter pilots based at Biggin Hill used to congregate at the Victorian White Hart pub further down the street.

WESTERHAM, THE GREEN c1955 W61015

As its name implies, this small town is the westernmost in Kent, almost on the border with Surrey. The green is dominated by the copper statue of General James Wolfe, the conqueror of Quebec in 1759, who was born at the local vicarage and spent his childhood here at the 17th-century building subsequently renamed Quebec House. The building is now owned and maintained by the National Trust.

WESTERHAM, MARKET SQUARE c1955 W61004

In the centre of the picture, the George and Dragon, with its quaint porch and balcony supported on brackets, was originally an old posting inn. The assize courts were held here when Maidstone, as the county town, was a considerable day's journey away.

IDE HILL, THE VILLAGE c1965 I49022

This small hamlet, with its modest houses clustered around a village green, was known as 'the dome of Kent' from a crown of beech trees surmounting its position high up on the sandstone ridge overlooking the Weald of Kent. The little general store, on the right, with its chewing gum machines and daily newspaper placards around the entrance, was a valued local amenity.

FOUR ELMS, THE VILLAGE c1960 F156009

As can be seen from the two television aerials sprouting above the rooftop on the right, modern innovations in home entertainment were already making their presence felt in the early sixties. This peaceful village lies below the slopes of the Greensand Hills. A cumbersome sit-up-and-beg bicycle with panniers on the back has been left leaning against one of the stone pillars around the small front garden of the house whose windows have been thrown open to the summer air.

EDENBRIDGE, HIGH STREET c1955 E21015

Even in the mid-fifties, Edenbridge retained some of its atmosphere as a small agricultural town, strung out along the Roman road which reached out across the Weald from Lewes to London. Its name was originally 'Eadhelm's bridge', so the River Eden is named from this crossing point and not the other way around. The signboard of the White Horse pub, across the road, advertises the availability of the locally-brewed Westerham ales.

EDENBRIDGE, MAIN ROAD c1955 E21042

Here we see another view of the long, straggling street with its delightful half-timbered cottages and the brick Baptist Chapel on the opposite side of the road.

TONBRIDGE
The Castle c1950 T101078
The formidable 13th-century gatehouse of the castle, with four
massive circular flanking towers and four portcullises in the
entrance, stands on the site of a former Saxon fortress. Richard de
Clare, a kinsman of William the Conqueror, initiated the castle's
construction in 1070. But the family, who were the most powerful
in England during the Middle Ages, were constantly in conflict
with the king, and the building was finally rendered indefensible by
the Parliamentarians during the Civil War. The adjoining Gothic
mansion was built by a Mr Hooker in 1793, and is now
a local government office.

TONBRIDGE, HIGH STREET 1948 T101021

Into the early fifties, the Capitol Theatre, on the left, still provided the residents of Tonbridge with a regularly changing programme of live entertainment, whilst the Red Lion Hotel on the right offered more intoxicating pleasures to its patrons. The adjoining premises were for many years a dairy, and the remnants of its painted sign are visible on the gable end above.

TONBRIDGE, HIGH STREET c1950 T101038

On the extreme right is the doorway of the timbered 16th-century Chequers Inn. A swinging sign, which was formerly suspended from the two hooks above the roadway, had allegedly been installed there during the reign of Elizabeth 1.

TONBRIDGE, HIGH STREET 1951
T101061
The crowded and busy pavements on both sides of the street, and the pedestrian crossing marked with belisha beacons in the middle of the photograph, show little indication of the enormous weight of motor traffic which this section of the main High Street had to bear; the construction of a by-pass brought an end to the regular bottlenecks and hold-ups.

PADDOCK WOOD, OAST HOUSES c1950 P220001

This collection of photographs was taken at what was, until recently, the Whitbread Hop Farm on the low-lying fields between Paddock Wood and Beltring; the photographs serve as a reminder of the important role hop-growing formerly occupied in Kent's agriculture. The hop plant, Humulus lupus, was probably introduced to England by the Flemish, although it was not used as a bittering agent in brewing until the end of the Middle Ages. At first it was a cottage crop, frowned on as a drug, and was grown up poles. But the 16th century saw beer, which incorporated hops in its ingredients, surpass ale in ▶

PADDOCK WOOD, LOADING HOPS FOR THE OAST HOUSES c1955 P220018

popularity; this led to the establishment of the Kentish hop gardens, mainly in a triangle formed by Maidstone, Tonbridge and Tenterden but with others around Sittingbourne and Canterbury. The first green climbing shoots appear in May, winding clockwise up strings attached to an overhead gantry of wire, and the pendulous yellow-green cones are usually harvested in early September. Up until the Second World War, this work was undertaken by entire families who came from South London and the East End to stay on the farms and supplement their income with this casual labour, but ▶

PADDOCK WOOD, MEASURING THE HOPS c1950 P220009

PADDOCK WOOD, UNLOADING THE POKES c1950 P220003

mechanisation replaced them in the post-war world. The unique oast houses are basically kilns, or ovens, where the piles of hops were dried on sacking laid over wooden slats, and heated by fires of anthracite mixed with sulphur. The resulting fumes escaped through the distinctively shaped cowls at the top. This process has also been modernised, and many of the old oast houses are now used as storerooms or converted, with difficulty, into houses.

PADDOCK WOOD, LOADING THE HOPS c1950 P220011

PADDOCK WOOD, HOP PICKING c1950 P220020

PEMBURY, HIGH STREET C1955 P266010
Pembury is now slowly being absorbed into the outskirts of Tunbridge Wells; it is situated on the main A21 London to Hastings road.

PEMBURY, HIGH STREET C1955 P266011
These two photographs of the village High Street give some indication of the constantly-flowing stream of traffic which passes the small, half-timbered Black Horse pub with its adjacent wine merchant and the large petrol station on the right-hand side of the picture.

SOUTHBOROUGH
High Street c1955 S152002

Gradually absorbed to become a suburb of
Tunbridge Wells over the first half of the 20th
century, this section of village shops and
businesses along the main highway running
between London and Eastbourne continued
to flourish. There is little to distinguish this
scene from one at the turn of the century,
except for the installation of the tall lamp
standards, the pedestrian crossing and the
parking restriction signs.

GROOMBRIDGE, THE VILLAGE c1960 G216042
The Kent-Sussex border divides the village in two, but this area, the older part with tile-hung cottages clustered around a triangular green, is in Kent. Its name is said to derive from a Saxon, Gromen (which translates simply as 'the man' or 'groom'), who built a moated castle where the 17th-century private house Groombridge Place now stands.

TUNBRIDGE WELLS, THE PANTILES c1955 T87009
Formerly called The Parade, this fashionable rendezvous and shopping parade was first laid out in 1638, taking its current name from the grey concave tiles with which it was paved in 1697 at the instigation of Queen Anne. They, in turn, were mainly replaced in 1793 by the large flagstones which we see today.

TUNBRIDGE WELLS, GROSVENOR ROAD 1961 T87067

We are looking along Grosvenor Road towards the A26 to Tonbridge and London from the town centre at Five Ways, with Mount Ephraim Road on the left. This photograph shows the remarkable range of architectural styles which are represented within this comparatively small shopping area.

TUNBRIDGE WELLS, MOUNT PLEASANT c1955 T87401

The carefully-pollarded lime trees along both sides of this north to south street help to shade the frontages of the varied shops and other retail establishments which flourish here. On the extreme left, the Cadena Coffee House evokes memories of one of the major pleasures of the 18th-century beau monde who flocked to this inland resort: coffee-drinking was possibly a welcome change from imbibing the chalybeate waters.

Index

Frith Book Co Titles

www.frithbook.co.uk

The Frith Book Company publishes over 100 new titles each year. A selection of those currently available are listed below. For latest catalogue please contact Frith Book Co.

Town Books 96pp, 100 photos. County and Themed Books 128pp, 150 photos (unless specified). All titles hardback laminated case and jacket except those indicated pb (paperback)

Around Bakewell	1-85937-113-2	£12.99	Around Great Yarmouth	1-85937-085-3	£12.99
Around Barnstaple	1-85937-084-5	£12.99	Around Guildford	1-85937-117-5	£12.99
Around Bath	1-85937-097-7	£12.99	Hampshire	1-85937-064-0	£14.99
Berkshire (pb)	1-85937-191-4	£9.99	Around Harrogate	1-85937-112-4	£12.99
Around Blackpool	1-85937-049-7	£12.99	Around Horsham	1-85937-127-2	£12.99
Around Bognor Regis	1-85937-055-1	£12.99	Around Ipswich	1-85937-133-7	£12.99
Around Bournemouth	1-85937-067-5	£12.99	Ireland (pb)	1-85937-181-7	£9.99
Brighton (pb)	1-85937-192-2	£8.99	Isle of Man	1-85937-065-9	£14.99
British Life A Century Ago	1-85937-103-5	£17.99	Isle of Wight	1-85937-114-0	£14.99
Buckinghamshire (pb)	1-85937-200-7	£9.99	Kent (pb)	1-85937-189-2	£9.99
Around Cambridge	1-85937-092-6	£12.99	Around Leicester	1-85937-073-x	£12.99
Cambridgeshire	1-85937-086-1	£14.99	Leicestershire (pb)	1-85937-185-x	£9.99
Canals and Waterways	1-85937-129-9	£17.99	Around Lincoln	1-85937-111-6	£12.99
Cheshire	1-85937-045-4	£14.99	Lincolnshire	1-85937-135-3	£14.99
Around Chester	1-85937-090-x	£12.99	London (pb)	1-85937-183-3	£9.99
Around Chichester	1-85937-089-6	£12.99	Around Maidstone	1-85937-056-x	£12.99
Churches of Berkshire	1-85937-170-1	£17.99	New Forest	1-85937-128-0	£14.99
Churches of Dorset	1-85937-172-8	£17.99	Around Newark	1-85937-105-1	£12.99
Colchester (pb)	1-85937-188-4	£8.99	Around Newquay	1-85937-140-x	£12.99
Cornwall	1-85937-054-3	£14.99	North Devon Coast	1-85937-146-9	£14.99
Cumbria	1-85937-101-9	£14.99	Northumberland and Tyne & Wear		
Dartmoor	1-85937-145-0	£14.99		1-85937-072-1	£14.99
Around Derby	1-85937-046-2	£12.99	Norwich (pb)	1-85937-194-9	£8.99
Derbyshire (pb)	1-85937-196-5	£9.99	Around Nottingham	1-85937-060-8	£12.99
Devon	1-85937-052-7	£14.99	Nottinghamshire (pb)	1-85937-187-6	£9.99
Dorset	1-85937-075-6	£14.99	Around Oxford	1-85937-096-9	£12.99
Dorset Coast	1-85937-062-4	£14.99	Oxfordshire	1-85937-076-4	£14.99
Down the Severn	1-85937-118-3	£14.99	Peak District	1-85937-100-0	£14.99
Down the Thames	1-85937-121-3	£14.99	Around Penzance	1-85937-069-1	£12.99
Around Dublin	1-85937-058-6	£12.99	Around Plymouth	1-85937-119-1	£12.99
East Sussex	1-85937-130-2	£14.99	Around St Ives	1-85937-068-3	£12.99
Around Eastbourne	1-85937-061-6	£12.99	Around Scarborough	1-85937-104-3	£12.99
Edinburgh (pb)	1-85937-193-0	£8.99	Scotland (pb)	1-85937-182-5	£9.99
English Castles	1-85937-078-0	£14.99	Scottish Castles	1-85937-077-2	£14.99
Essex	1-85937-082-9	£14.99	Around Sevenoaks and Tonbridge		
Around Exeter	1-85937-126-4	£12.99		1-85937-057-8	£12.99
Exmoor	1-85937-132-9	£14.99	Around Southampton	1-85937-088-8	£12.99
Around Falmouth	1-85937-066-7	£12.99	Around Southport	1-85937-106-x	£12.99

Available from your local bookshop or from the publisher

Frith Book Co Titles (continued)

Around Shrewsbury	1-85937-110-8	£12.99
Shropshire	1-85937-083-7	£14.99
South Devon Coast	1-85937-107-8	£14.99
South Devon Living Memories		
	1-85937-168-x	£14.99
Staffordshire (96pp)	1-85937-047-0	£12.99
Stone Circles & Ancient Monuments		
	1-85937-143-4	£17.99
Around Stratford upon Avon		
	1-85937-098-5	£12.99
Sussex (pb)	1-85937-184-1	£9.99

Around Torbay	1-85937-063-2	£12.99
Around Truro	1-85937-147-7	£12.99
Victorian & Edwardian Kent		
	1-85937-149-3	£14.99
Victorian & Edwardian Yorkshire		
	1-85937-154-x	£14.99
Warwickshire (pb)	1-85937-203-1	£9.99
Welsh Castles	1-85937-120-5	£14.99
West Midlands	1-85937-109-4	£14.99
West Sussex	1-85937-148-5	£14.99
Wiltshire	1-85937-053-5	£14.99
Around Winchester	1-85937-139-6	£12.99

Frith Book Co titles available Autumn 2000

Croydon Living Memories (pb)			
	1-85937-162-0	£9.99	Aug
Glasgow (pb)	1-85937-190-6	£9.99	Aug
Hertfordshire (pb)	1-85937-247-3	£9.99	Aug
North London	1-85937-206-6	£14.99	Aug
Victorian & Edwardian Maritime Album			
	1-85937-144-2	£17.99	Aug
Victorian Seaside	1-85937-159-0	£17.99	Aug
Cornish Coast	1-85937-163-9	£14.99	Sep
County Durham	1-85937-123-x	£14.99	Sep
Dorset Living Memories	1-85937-210-4	£14.99	Sep
Gloucestershire	1-85937-102-7	£14.99	Sep
Herefordshire	1-85937-174-4	£14.99	Sep
Kent Living Memories	1-85937-125-6	£14.99	Sep
Leeds (pb)	1-85937-202-3	£9.99	Sep
Ludlow (pb)	1-85937-176-0	£9.99	Sep
Norfolk (pb)	1-85937-195-7	£9.99	Sep
Somerset	1-85937-153-1	£14.99	Sep
Tees Valley & Cleveland	1-85937-211-2	£14.99	Sep
Thanet (pb)	1-85937-116-7	£9.99	Sep
Tiverton (pb)	1-85937-178-7	£9.99	Sep
Weymouth (pb)	1-85937-209-0	£9.99	Sep

Worcestershire	1-85937-152-3	£14.99	Sep
Yorkshire Living Memories	1-85937-166-3	£14.99	Sep
British Life A Century Ago (pb)			
	1-85937-213-9	£9.99	Oct
Camberley (pb)	1-85937-222-8	£9.99	Oct
Cardiff (pb)	1-85937-093-4	£9.99	Oct
Carmarthenshire	1-85937-216-3	£14.99	Oct
Cornwall (pb)	1-85937-229-5	£9.99	Oct
English Country Houses	1-85937-161-2	£17.99	Oct
Humberside	1-85937-215-5	£14.99	Oct
Lancashire (pb)	1-85937-197-3	£9.99	Oct
Liverpool (pb)	1-85937-234-1	£9.99	Oct
Manchester (pb)	1-85937-198-1	£9.99	Oct
Middlesex	1-85937-158-2	£14.99	Oct
Norfolk Living Memories	1-85937-217-1	£14.99	Oct
Preston (pb)	1-85937-212-0	£9.99	Oct
South Hams	1-85937-220-1	£14.99	Oct
Suffolk	1-85937-221-x	£9.99	Oct
Swansea (pb)	1-85937-167-1	£9.99	Oct
Victorian and Edwardian Sussex			
	1-85937-157-4	£14.99	Oct
West Yorkshire (pb)	1-85937-201-5	£9.99	Oct

See Frith books on the internet www.frithbook.co.uk

FRITH PRODUCTS & SERVICES

Francis Frith would doubtless be pleased to know that the pioneering publishing venture he started in 1860 still continues today. A hundred and forty years later, The Francis Frith Collection continues in the same innovative tradition and is now one of the foremost publishers of vintage photographs in the world. Some of the current activities include:

Interior Decoration

Today Frith's photographs can be seen framed and as giant wall murals in thousands of pubs, restaurants, hotels, banks, retail stores and other public buildings throughout the country. In every case they enhance the unique local atmosphere of the places they depict and provide reminders of gentler days in an increasingly busy and frenetic world.

Product Promotions

Frith products are used by many major companies to promote the sales of their own products or to reinforce their own history and heritage. Frith promotions have been used by Hovis bread, Courage beers, Scots Porage Oats, Colman's mustard, Cadbury's foods, Mellow Birds coffee, Dunhill pipe tobacco, Guinness, and Bulmer's Cider.

Genealogy and Family History

As the interest in family history and roots grows world-wide, more and more people are turning to Frith's photographs of Great Britain for images of the towns, villages and streets where their ancestors lived; and, of course, photographs of the churches and chapels where their ancestors were christened, married and buried are an essential part of every genealogy tree and family album.

Frith Products

All Frith photographs are available Framed or just as Mounted Prints and Posters (size 23 x 16 inches). These may be ordered from the address below. From time to time other products - Address Books, Calendars, Table Mats, etc - are available.

The Internet

Already twenty thousand Frith photographs can be viewed and purchased on the internet. By the end of the year 2000 some 60,000 Frith photographs will be available on the internet. The number of sites is constantly expanding, each focussing on different products and services from the Collection.
The main Frith sites are listed below.

www.francisfrith.co.uk
www.frithbook.co.uk

See the complete list of Frith Books at:
www.frithbook.co.uk
This web site is regularly updated with the latest list of publications from the Frith Book Company. If you wish to buy books relating to another part of the country that your local bookshop does not stock, you may purchase on-line.

For further information, trade, or author enquiries please contact us at the address below:
The Francis Frith Collection, Frith's Barn, Teffont, Salisbury, Wiltshire, England SP3 5QP.
Tel: +44 (0)1722 716 376 Fax: +44 (0)1722 716 881   Email: uksales@francisfrith.com

See Frith books on the internet www.frithbook.co.uk

TO RECEIVE YOUR FREE MOUNTED PRINT

Mounted Print
Overall size 14 x 11 inches

Cut out this Voucher and return it with your remittance for £1.50 to cover postage and handling, to UK addresses. For overseas addresses please include £4.00 post and handling. Choose any photograph included in this book. Your SEPIA print will be A4 in size, and mounted in a cream mount with burgundy rule lines, overall size 14 x 11 inches.

Order additional Mounted Prints at HALF PRICE (only £7.49 each*)

If there are further pictures you would like to order, possibly as gifts for friends and family, purchase them at half price (no additional postage and handling required).

Have your Mounted Prints framed*

For an additional £14.95 per print you can have your chosen Mounted Print framed in an elegant polished wood and gilt moulding, overall size 16 x 13 inches (no additional postage and handling required).

---

* IMPORTANT!
These special prices are only available if ordered using the original voucher on this page (no copies permitted) and at the same time as your free Mounted Print, for delivery to the same address

---

Frith Collectors' Guild

From time to time we publish a magazine of news and stories about Frith photographs and further special offers of Frith products. If you would like 12 months FREE membership, please return this form.

Send completed forms to:
The Francis Frith Collection, Frith's Barn, Teffont, Salisbury, Wiltshire SP3 5QP

Voucher for **FREE** and Reduced Price Frith Prints

Picture no.	Page number	Qty	Mounted @ £7.49	Framed + £14.95	Total Cost
		1	Free of charge*	£	£
			£7.49	£	£
			£7.49	£	£
			£7.49	£	£
			£7.49	£	£
			£7.49	£	£

Please allow 28 days for delivery	*** Post & handling**	**£1.50**
Book Title	**Total Order Cost**	**£**

Please do not photocopy this voucher. Only the original is valid, so please cut it out and return it to us.

I enclose a cheque / postal order for £ . . . . made payable to 'The Francis Frith Collection' OR please debit my Mastercard / Visa / Switch / Amex card

Number . . . .

Issue No(Switch only) . . . . .Valid from (Amex/Switch) . . . .

Expires . . . . Signature . . . .

Name Mr/Mrs/Ms . . . .

Address . . . .

. . . .

. . . .

. . . . Postcode . . . .

Daytime Tel No . . . . Valid to 31/12/02

The Francis Frith Collectors' Guild

Please enrol me as a member for 12 months free of charge.

Name Mr/Mrs/Ms . . . .

Address . . . .

. . . .

. . . .

. . . . Postcode . . . .

Free Print - see overleaf